Nine Days To

WELCOME PEACE

Nine Days To

WELCOME PEACE

JACQUES PHILIPPE

Scepter

Nine days to…

Collection edited by Timothée Berthon

The "Nine Days to" collection offers a guided retreat to be lived at home or on vacation, in the subway or on the train, for people who have little time but wish to devote ten minutes a day to spiritual growth.

Each book in the collection offers nine days of inspiring meditations that surround a specific theme for advancement in the spiritual life. Each serves as both a school of prayer and an authentic tool of self-transformation.

Two meditations are offered for each day. One can be experienced in the morning and the other at any opportune moment during the day or evening.

The journey includes reflection exercises, the Word of God, a meditation from a saint or another great spiritual author, and a resolution— all geared to help the participant dive into an authentic spiritual experience.

JACQUES PHILIPPE

Published by Scepter Publishers, Inc.
Info@scepterpublishers.org
www.scepterpublishers.org
800-322-8773
New York

Text and cover by Rose Design
Cover image: Nicole Baster on Unsplash

Library of Congress Control Number: 2019948659

PB ISBN: 9781594173653
eBook ISBN: 9781594173660

Printed in the United States of America

Contents

First Day

THE URGENCY
OF INTERIOR PEACE

Daily Mediation

INVITATION TO CONTEMPLATION

I compose myself, present to the current moment, and I breathe calmly. With the eyes of faith, I put myself in God's view, that of the Father of Heaven who loves me tenderly. I am attentive to God's presence in my heart. I contemplate for several minutes.

SIGN OF THE CROSS

In the name of the Father, and of the Son, and of the Holy Spirit. Amen.

PRAYER TO THE HOLY SPIRIT

Holy Spirit, you who are the light, you who are the consoler, come guide my prayer this day. Make me know the beauty and depth of divine love. Come establish God's peace in my heart and make me capable of spreading this peace around me.

MEDITATION FROM
FR. JACQUES PHILIPPE

The grace for which we are going to ask during this retreat is the grace to receive God's peace in our heart in a deeper and more abundant way, and to be able to transmit this peace around us.

It's the seventh beatitude from Matthew's Gospel: "Blessed are the peacemakers, for they shall be called sons of God" (Mt 5:9).

Clearly, we can only transmit peace if it resides in us.

In the Letter to the Colossians, St. Paul puts it this way: "Let the peace of Christ rule in your hearts, to which indeed you were called in the one body" (Col 3:15).

According to St. Paul, then, it is truly a call to welcome God's peace which He offers to us. To be at peace is an essential element of the Christian vocation.

This call is particularly strong today, in a world so stricken with fear, agitation, and worry. There is a true spiritual urgency that we receive and transmit God's peace.

The primary obligation of a Christian is not to be perfect, nor to resolve all our problems, nor to succeed. It is to be at peace.

I think of Etty Hillesum, the young Jewish woman who lived in Amsterdam during the Second World War and who experienced a beautiful encounter with God. In 1942, when the Nazi persecution cracked down on Amsterdam, here's what she expressed in her diary:

> Our only moral obligation is to recultivate vast fields of peace within ourselves, and to extend them little by little until this peace ripples out towards others. And the more peace there is in others, the more there will be in the world in abundance.[1]

The more the world is in crisis, the more important it is that our hearts be at peace.

In the Book of Isaiah, when Jerusalem is menaced by enemies, the people are worried and struggle to find political solutions. Here are the words that the Prophet says to them:

---

1. Etty Hillesum, *Une vie bouleversée*, Collection Points (Paris: Éditions du Seuil, 1981), p. 169.

For thus said the Lord God, the Holy One of Israel: By waiting and by calm you shall be saved, in quiet and in trust shall be your strength. But this you did not will (Is 30:15, NABRE translation).

If our hearts are inhabited by peace and trust, we will lean on the Lord, and we will find all the right responses to our difficulties. We will find constructive solutions, decisions guided by love for the questions that confront us.

On the other hand, if we let worry and fear invade our hearts, we risk reacting poorly to the events facing us: we close ourselves off, we flee, we become aggressive or violent, or we make precipitous decisions that not only don't resolve anything, but sometimes even augment the bad instead of diminishing it.

PRAYER

Let us put our trust in the Virgin Mary, the Queen of Peace:

> Hail Mary, full of grace, the Lord is with thee. Blessed art thou among women and blessed is the fruit of thy womb, Jesus. Holy Mary, Mother of God, pray for us, sinners, now and at the hour of our death. Amen.
>
> May the all-powerful and merciful God bless us and keep us, He who is Father, Son and Holy Spirit. Amen.

A GRACE TO REQUEST

I ask myself this question: What do I diffuse around me? Peace and trust? Or agitation and worry? I ask God for grace, that his peace should live in me, and that I may become a true peacemaker.

LIGHT FROM A FAITHFUL WITNESS

"The more a being lives in the most intimate recollection of his soul, the stronger this radiance that comes from him and that attracts all others to his side."

> —St. Teresa Benedicta of the Cross, OCD
> (Edith Stein)

MEDITATE ON THE WORD

I read and meditate on the passage from Isaiah cited above:

> For thus said the Lord God, the Holy One of Israel, "In returning and rest you shall be saved; in quietness and in trust shall be your strength." And you would not [accept] (Is 30:15).

I keep this phrase in my heart and I try to repeat it often throughout the day:

"In quietness and in trust shall be your strength."

Second Day

PEACE, A GIFT FROM GOD

Daily Meditation

INVITATION TO CONTEMPLATION

I compose myself, present to the current moment, and I breathe calmly. With the eyes of faith, I put myself in God's view, that of the Father of Heaven who loves me tenderly. I am attentive to God's presence in my heart. I contemplate for several minutes.

SIGN OF THE CROSS

In the name of the Father, and of the Son, and of the Holy Spirit. Amen.

PRAYER TO THE HOLY SPIRIT

Holy Spirit, you who are the light, you who are the consoler, come guide my prayer this day. Make me know the beauty and depth of divine love. Come establish God's peace in my heart and make me capable of spreading this peace around me.

MEDITATION FROM
FR. JACQUES PHILIPPE

The Lord calls us to be at peace and to transmit this peace around us; this is how we will be truly children of God.

This peace that must inhabit our hearts is, above all, a gift from God. Of course, some effort is required on our part; there's certainly work to accomplish. That work is what we'll consider over the next few days. Above all, however, peace is a gift to be welcomed, a grace to request and to receive. Only God truly can communicate peace to us; our human efforts are insufficient.

It's good to meditate on the Scriptural texts that speak to us about peace as a gift from God.

The most significant passages are found in John's Gospel, in the Lord's discourse after the Last Supper.

After having washed the feet of his disciples, Jesus spoke to them for a long time during this last meal that he shared with them. He leaves them with his spiritual testament, in a way, before entering into his Passion.

At the beginning of chapter 14, we find these words: "Let not your hearts be troubled; believe in God, believe also in me" (Jn 14:1).

The disciples are upset and worried because of everything going on in Jerusalem, plus the hostility against Jesus that was getting stronger and stronger.

The first thing that Jesus asks of them is to calm down: They must not let themselves get upset and must keep an attitude of faith.

Jesus asks this of them so that they can hear all the important things he has to say to them.

An upset heart is often incapable of hearing God's Word, while a peaceful heart allows it to penetrate deeply.

A little later, Jesus speaks to them about the coming of the Holy Spirit, and we find this magnificent promise: "Peace I leave with you; my peace I give to you; not as the world gives do I give to you. Let not your hearts be troubled, neither let them be afraid" (Jn 14:27).

Jesus will soon leave his disciples, but he promises them the grace of the Holy Spirit, and he leaves them this precious gift of peace.

The peace that Jesus promises is not the peace of this world. It's not the tranquility of everything going well, of problems resolved and desires satisfied, which would be a peace that is fairly rare. The peace that Jesus promises us is a peace that can be experienced even in difficult and uncertain situations because it has its source and foundation in God.

At the conclusion of his long discourse, at the end of chapter 16, his last words invoke the theme of peace again: "I have said this to you, that in me you may have peace. In the world you have tribulation; but be of good cheer, I have overcome the world" (Jn 16:33). It seems as if the ultimate goal of all these words that Jesus tells his disciples is to establish them in peace.

They must find peace in the certainty of Christ's victory over all the evil forces that upset the world: "Be of good cheer, I have overcome the world."

At the same time, Jesus shows us what the secret of peace is, the true source of peace: Our peace is the peace of Jesus.

Such is union with Jesus: Listening to his Word, faith, trust, prayer and love allow us to welcome into our hearts God's peace.

PRAYER

Let us put our trust in the Virgin Mary, the Queen of Peace:

> Hail Mary, full of grace, the Lord is with thee. Blessed art thou among women and blessed is the fruit of thy womb, Jesus. Holy Mary, Mother of God, pray for us, sinners, now and at the hour of our death. Amen.

> May the all-powerful and merciful God bless us and keep us, he who is Father, Son and Holy Spirit. Amen.

A GRACE TO REQUEST

I understand better that true peace finds its source in Jesus.

I ask for the grace to live more in union with him, spending less time ruminating on what worries and troubles me, and more time thinking of Jesus, accepting his words, and praying to him.

LIGHT FROM A FAITHFUL WITNESS

"You have made us for you, Lord, and our hearts are restless unless they rest in you."

—St. Augustine

"Peace is the grace of all graces, the gift of God, a cyclone stronger than any storm."

—Fr. Marie-Dominique Molinié, OP

MEDITATE ON THE WORD

I read and meditate on the passage from the Gospel of John cited above:

> Peace I leave with you; my peace I give to you; not as the world gives do I give to you. Let not your hearts be troubled, neither let them be afraid (Jn 14:27).

Third Day

THE MORE PEACEFUL I AM,
THE MORE GOD ACTS

Daily Meditation

INVITATION TO CONTEMPLATION

I compose myself, present to the current moment, and I breathe calmly. With the eyes of faith, I put myself in God's view, that of the Father of Heaven who loves me tenderly. I am attentive to God's presence in my heart. I contemplate for several minutes.

SIGN OF THE CROSS

In the name of the Father, and of the Son, and of the Holy Spirit. Amen.

PRAYER TO THE HOLY SPIRIT

Holy Spirit, you who are the light, you who are the consoler, come guide my prayer this day. Make me know the beauty and depth of divine love. Come establish God's peace in my heart and make me capable of spreading this peace around me.

MEDITATION FROM
FR. JACQUES PHILIPPE

The search for interior peace is more than just aspiring for psychological tranquility. It's something much more profound: It's about opening ourselves to God's action.

We must understand one truth that's simple but of great spiritual significance: The more we tend towards peace, the more the grace of God can act in our lives.

St. Seraphim of Sarov, one of the greatest saints from Russia, said this: "Acquire the Spirit of Peace, and a thousand souls around you will be saved!"[1]

Like a peaceful lake perfectly reflects the sun, so a peaceful spirit is receptive to the action and the movements of the Holy Spirit.

Lorenzo Scupoli, a sixteenth century spiritual writer, said: "The devil does his utmost to banish peace from one's heart, because he

---

1. Translation taken from *http://orthochristian.com/63166.html*.

knows that God abides in peace and it is in peace that He accomplishes great things."[2]

St. Francis de Sales says the same thing to one of his protégés. "Because love can only reside in peace, always be careful to keep the holy tranquility of heart that I so often recommend to you."[3]

Trying to keep the peace of our hearts and fighting against worry, trouble, and spiritual agitation are indispensable conditions for letting God act, thus allowing us to grow in love and in giving our lives over to the fruitfulness to which we're called.

I would add that it's only in peace that we can discern rightly. When we're not at peace, when we're filled with worry, agitation, or trouble, that's when we're at the mercy of our emotions, and we don't have an objective or accurate outlook.

---

2. Translation taken from *Searching for and Maintaining Peace* by Jacques Philippe, p. 11.

3. Letter CCXXXVI to Madame la Présidente Favre, November 18, 1612.

Sometimes we are tempted to see everything darkly, and to doubt everything in our lives. On the contrary, when we're at peace, we see clearly.

St. Ignatius of Loyola understood this well, too. He distinguishes periods of "consolation" and of "desolation" in the spiritual life, and he invites us not to make decisions concerning our life during the latter, when we're going through troubled times. We must simply remain faithful to what we decided during the last period of peace. We must wait for peace to come back again before making a life-changing decision.

We should, then, deduce this rule of conduct: When a problem comes up that makes us lose our peace, the urgency is not in resolving the problem in the hope of regaining peace; rather, the urgency is in first recovering some minimum amount of peace, and then seeing what we can do with the problem.

Thus, we avoid making hasty or precipitous choices governed by fear, and we avoid trying to resolve problems that are out of our power at any cost, which is what happens sometimes.

How can we recover this minimum of peace? We do this essentially by trusting in God with fervent prayer, by making acts of faith and hope, and by recalling the words of Scripture that invite us to greater trust.

PRAYER

Let us put our trust in the Virgin Mary, the Queen of Peace:

> Hail Mary, full of grace, the Lord is with thee. Blessed art thou among women and blessed is the fruit of thy womb, Jesus. Holy Mary, Mother of God, pray for us, sinners, now and at the hour of our death. Amen.

> May the all-powerful and merciful God bless us and keep us, he who is Father, Son and Holy Spirit. Amen.

A GRACE REQUEST

I understand better that it's not in upsetting or worrying myself that I will resolve problems, but in remaining trusting and peaceful as much as possible. I ask of God the grace to help me in this endeavor.

LIGHT FROM A FAITHFUL WITNESS

"When it pleased God to create the universe, he worked in a void, and look at what beautiful things he did! In the same way, if he wants to work in us to make things infinitely above the natural beauties that came from his hands, he doesn't need us to move much to help him . . . rather, let him do it; he is pleased to work in the void. Keep yourselves in peace and tranquility before him, and simply follow the movement that he gives us. . . . Let us keep then our souls in peace and our spiritual power at rest before him while waiting for all movement and all life to come from him alone."[4]

—Ven. Francis Mary Paul Libermann, CSSp

---

4. Letter XLVI to a seminary director, September 11, 1837.

MEDITATE ON THE WORD

In his Letter to the Philippians, St. Paul writes:

> The Lord is at hand. Have no anxiety about anything, but in everything by prayer and supplication with thanksgiving let your requests be made known to God. And the peace of God, which passes all understanding, will keep your hearts and your minds in Christ Jesus (Phil 4:5–7).

I take time to stay with this passage, reading it several times and meditating on it. I let it descend into my heart and I let the Word of God transform me.

"The Lord is at hand. Have no anxiety about anything."

Fourth Day

Prayer, A Place for Peace

Daily Meditation

INVITATION TO CONTEMPLATION

I compose myself, present to the current moment, and I breathe calmly. With the eyes of faith, I put myself in God's view, that of the Father of Heaven who loves me tenderly. I am attentive to God's presence in my heart. I contemplate for several minutes.

SIGN OF THE CROSS

In the name of the Father, and of the Son, and of the Holy Spirit. Amen.

PRAYER TO THE HOLY SPIRIT

Holy Spirit, you who are the light, you who are the consoler, come guide my prayer this day. Make me know the beauty and depth of divine love. Come establish God's peace in my heart and make me capable of spreading this peace around me.

MEDITATION FROM
FR. JACQUES PHILIPPE

One of the fundamental ways of acquiring interior peace is faithfulness to prayer.

Very often, we lack peace because we don't pray sufficiently. Our peace doesn't find its source simply in human realities; it finds its source in God, and that's where we should look for it.

The more we are in communication with God, the more we find peace.

A contemporary Egyptian Monk, Matta el Meskeen (Matthew the Poor), says this in one of his books on prayer: "Every day, in prayer, God gives us an all-new peace."

This is a beautiful reality. In God there is an energy, a fantastic life, but there's also a very profound peace. St. Paul often speaks of God as the "God of peace" (see Thessalonians and other books written by St. Paul).

God is an abyss of peace, an ocean of peace. Each time that we are in real contact with him, some of this divine peace descends into our hearts.

We've all had this experience at one time or another. For example, I may be very anxious about something, and it leaves me feeling troubled and worried. I go to spend an hour of adoration before the Blessed Sacrament, or I spend twenty minutes to say my rosary calmly, and at the end of this prayer time I feel more tranquil.

The overall situation is the same, it hasn't changed; but I'm different, my heart is more at rest. Very simply, even though this prayer may be very simple and very poorly done, it was done with faith, and it has put me in contact with God, thus a parcel of God's peace has come to rest in my heart.

Sometimes, it's a "river of peace," like the Scripture says (see Is 48:18), that prayer gives us. Sometimes it's simply little drops: I'm still suffering, I'm not completely tranquil psychologically, but some drops of God's peace have entered my heart, the "spark of the soul," as the spiritual authors[1] say, and that suffices for

---

1. St. Jerome introduces the concept in his commentary on the Book of Ezekiel, which is then most notably expounded upon by St. Albert the Great, St. Thomas Aquinas, Master Eckhart, St. Bonaventure, and St. Francis de Sales.

me to live through things differently, for me to be more confident and stronger in facing situations.

This faithfulness to prayer is an urgency today. It's not really in front of the television, or in browsing the internet, or in endless conversations with others that we find peace: Often, actually, these things leave us more agitated than before.

Conversely, before the Blessed Sacrament, in front of Jesus, we always find a modicum of peace that we need. It is enough to take the necessary time, to be before him with an attitude of faith and hope to be poor in spirit and expect everything from God's mercy—and he will visit us.

Sometimes it's an obligation for us to take the time to pray until we regain our peace, and thereby not to make our fears and worries weigh on others. It's a requirement of being charitable.

It is particularly necessary to take this time if our prayer is often nourished by Holy Scripture. There are moments in life when only the Word of God has enough force, enough authority, to permit us to regain the peace that we have

lost. Our human reason is sometimes insufficient, but the Word of God is effective.

Prayer

Let us put our trust in the Virgin Mary, the
Queen of Peace:

> Hail Mary, full of grace, the Lord is with thee.
> Blessed art thou among women and blessed
> is the fruit of thy womb, Jesus. Holy Mary,
> Mother of God, pray for us, sinners, now and
> at the hour of our death. Amen.

> May the all-powerful and merciful God bless
> us and keep us, he who is Father, Son and
> Holy Spirit. Amen.

A Grace to Request

I ask God for the grace to be more faithful to
prayer and, each time I need it, to know to spend
more time in the presence of the Lord in order to
receive the gift of peace. May I truly learn through
prayer to unburden all my cares unto God.

Light from a Faithful Witness

"The greatest ways to establish the admirable reign of Jesus in us are precisely the spirit of continual prayer and peace of the soul. Ceaselessly remind yourself and fix yourself solidly on this truth in your spirit and in your heart, that the greatest way, the infallible way, even, of achieving this continual prayer, is to possess your soul in peace before Our Lord."

—Ven. François-Marie-Paul
Libermann, CSSp

"Who can describe the gifts of truth, peace, strength, consolation and hope that prayer can place and let loose within a soul!"

—Ven. Marthe Robin

Meditate on the Word

In his first letter, the Apostle Peter wrote: "Cast all your anxieties on him, for he cares about you" (1 Pt 5:7).

I keep this phrase in my heart, and I repeat it often over the course of today.

"Cast all your anxieties on him, for he cares about you."

Fifth Day

Peace, Fruit of Trust

Daily Meditation

INVITATION TO CONTEMPLATION

I compose myself, present to the current moment, and I breathe calmly. With the eyes of faith, I put myself in God's view, that of the Father of Heaven who loves me tenderly. I am attentive to God's presence in my heart. I contemplate for several minutes.

SIGN OF THE CROSS

In the name of the Father, and of the Son, and of the Holy Spirit. Amen.

PRAYER TO THE HOLY SPIRIT

Holy Spirit, you who are the light, you who are the consoler, come guide my prayer this day. Make me know the beauty and depth of divine love. Come establish God's peace in my heart and make me capable of spreading this peace around me.

MEDITATION FROM
FR. JACQUES PHILIPPE

If our desire during this retreat is to receive God's peace, we must ask ourselves this question: What are the essential conditions for being at peace?

It seems to me that there are two essential elements that complement each other, elements that can't be separated from each other.

The first is trust, an absolute trust in the mercy of God and in his fidelity. This trust isn't always easy to practice, of course. We don't always have sensory proof of God's love, and life sometimes brings us the heavy burden of suffering and disillusion.

But this trust is necessary. And even if God leads us on paths that aren't always those we would want, he never betrays our trust. "Hope does not disappoint us," St. Paul says in his letter to the Romans (5:5).

The principal enemy of our peace is not exterior circumstances or attitudes of others, it's our lack of faith and trust in God, which makes us lose our certainty that he can draw good out of anything, and that he will never abandon us.

If we truly had faith, every difficult thing that happened to us wouldn't be able to trouble our peace. The mountains of worry that sometimes come would be quickly thrown into the sea.

The second essential condition for peace of heart is telling God "yes" without hesitation, which means completely opening our hearts to him and being determined to refuse nothing to God. That doesn't mean that we must be perfect all of a sudden; that is impossible, of course.

But simply, we must let God have full permission to enter into our life and lead it as he desires.

To desire the will of God in all things isn't always easy. We are often attacked by fear, precisely because we lack this faith and trust. We don't believe enough that God wants our happiness.

Sometimes we have a terrible fear of giving ourselves completely to God because we don't know where that will lead us, and we would prefer to remain masters of our destiny, to be sure that everything goes according to our desires.

But this is a bad calculation. We don't really know what is good for ourselves. Only God knows. It's better to trust him and leave ourselves in his hands.

Notice also one thing: Everything in our life that was not given by God will sooner or later become a source of worry.

We are then left to manage it by ourselves, with our own resources, our own light, and in the end, it could create a lot of anxiety for us.

On the contrary, if we have given everything to God, we are freed from this burden of having to resolve everything by ourselves. It's the Lord who will take care of it, and he'll do it better than we can.

Let us remind ourselves of the beautiful words of Jesus in the Gospel of St. Matthew:

> Come to me, all who labor and are heavy laden, and I will give you rest. Take my yoke upon you, and learn from me; for I am gentle and lowly in heart, and you will find rest for your souls. For my yoke is easy, and my burden is light (Mt 11:28–30).

Life is lighter and simpler when we have given everything to God.

When we seek only God, we are always at peace. By contrast, those who look to themselves, who want to manage and control their existence on their own, are loaded down with heavy cares. One of the great enemies of interior peace is the attachment to our own ideas and to our own will. On the contrary, detachment is the source of peace.

Of course, we have the right to desire and want things, but we must always retain a certain freedom of heart, without worrying if things don't go as we may have wished.

This detachment is itself founded on trust. God knows better than we do what will make us grow, and he wants our true happiness even more than we do.

The bigger the trust, the more we will be free, and the more we will find peace.

Prayer

Let us put our trust in the Virgin Mary, the Queen of Peace:

> Hail Mary, full of grace, the Lord is with thee. Blessed art thou among women and blessed is the fruit of thy womb, Jesus. Holy Mary, Mother of God, pray for us, sinners, now and at the hour of our death. Amen.

> May the all-powerful and merciful God bless us and keep us, he who is Father, Son and Holy Spirit. Amen.

A Grace to Request

I ask God for the grace of a greater trust in his love, such that I can be firmly decided always to say "yes" to him.

Light from a Faithful Witness

"Ah! If we knew that the Spirit put happiness and peace in a soul that abandons itself to God, and all that he removes of useless suffering, we would genuflect out of happiness, admiration, and recognition."

—Ven. Marthe Robin

"If we could, with a single interior glance, see all the generosity and mercy in God's designs for each of us, even in what we call disgrace, sorrow, or affliction, our happiness would be such that we'd throw ourselves into the arms of the Divine Will with the abandon of a young child throwing itself into the arms of its mother. We would act, in all things, with the intention of pleasing God. Then we would be in a holy repose, persuaded that God is our Father, and that he desires our salvation more than we desire it ourselves."

—St. Marie of the Incarnation, OSU

"God knows what he wants to do with me, I have no worries on the subject."

—St. Teresa Benedicta of the Cross, OCD

MEDITATE ON THE WORD

I repeat this passage from St. Matthew's Gospel, from the reflection today:

> Come to me, all who labor and are heavy laden, and I will give you rest. Take my yoke upon you, and learn from me; for I am gentle and lowly in heart, and you will find rest for your souls. For my yoke is easy, and my burden is light (Mt 11:28–30).

I keep this phrase in my heart and I repeat it often during the day:

"Take my yoke upon you, and learn from me; for I am gentle and lowly in heart, and you will find rest for your souls."

Sixth Day

HUMILITY, SOURCE OF PEACE

Daily Meditation

INVITATION TO CONTEMPLATION

I compose myself, present to the current moment, and I breathe calmly. With the eyes of faith, I put myself in God's view, that of the Father of Heaven who loves me tenderly. I am attentive to God's presence in my heart. I contemplate for several minutes.

SIGN OF THE CROSS

In the name of the Father, and of the Son, and of the Holy Spirit. Amen.

PRAYER TO THE HOLY SPIRIT

Holy Spirit, you who are the light, you who are the consoler, come guide my prayer this day. Make me know the beauty and depth of divine love. Come establish God's peace in my heart and make me capable of spreading this peace around me.

MEDITATION FROM
FR. JACQUES PHILIPPE

Arriving at the sixth day of our retreat, let's try to understand what the enemies of peace are, let's find those things that stop us from welcoming God's peace.

We are interested today in one of peace's greatest enemies: pride.

People who are motivated by pride will never find true peace. They think they're better than the others, they're filled with judgment or disdain, and they pretend to be self-sufficient and capable of doing everything better than others.

They also want to control and manage their lives according to their own wisdom, which they estimate as the best, and load themselves up with big concerns such as we already saw.

What's more, they experience more dramatically every failure, every situation that reveals their limits, their errors, or their weaknesses. They always feel menaced, always feel obliged to defend their image and their brand.

These people have the pretention of presenting a perfect image of themselves without faults, which winds up being a heavy weight. They are constantly asking themselves the following worried question: "What do others think of me?" They often consider others as rivals or as threats.

There is a great risk of enclosing themselves in perfectionism, a pretense of doing everything perfectly and of being the best in everything, which creates constant stress. This perfectionism is one of the worst enemies of peace of heart.

How different is the attitude of humble people! When they are confronted with their limits, their weaknesses, and their errors, they accept them peaceably. When something happens that shows that they're imperfect or when they fall into some error, they are neither despondent nor discouraged, but remain tranquil. These people get up right away and throw themselves with trust into the arms of the good Lord.

They have put all their hope in the mercy of God, not in themselves. They accept with simplicity that they are capable of falling, of making mistakes, and that they need forgiveness.

These people accept not being in a position to save themselves, but rather that of receiving salvation as a free gift of God's mercy. They are even happy to depend entirely on God's bounty.

Prideful people will always be at war with someone. They are at war with God because they refuse to let themselves be led like little children and be molded by the wisdom of God. They're at war with others because of jealousy, or because they disdain them or see them as rivals; they are always in competition with others, which, in the end, is really tiring.

They will be at war within themselves because they don't accept the weakness or poverty that exists in every person. They will also be at war with life because they pretend to be successful in everything, refusing any circumstance that unveils their poverty, weakness, or fragility.

Humble people will be at peace with God: They submit to him and let him educate them like children. They will be at peace with others because they accept others as they are and remain open towards them, not in competition with anybody.

These people will be at peace with themselves because they accept their own weaknesses and imperfections, and they aren't worried about their faults or falls.

They will be at peace with life because they have no pretenses about controlling or dominating everything, but know how to welcome reality as it is and abandon themselves to God's hands.

PRAYER

Let us put our trust in the Virgin Mary, the Queen of Peace:

Hail Mary, full of grace, the Lord is with thee. Blessed art thou among women and blessed is the fruit of thy womb, Jesus. Holy Mary, Mother of God, pray for us, sinners, now and at the hour of our death. Amen.

May the all-powerful and merciful God bless us and keep us, he who is Father, Son and Holy Spirit. Amen.

A Grace to Request

I ask God for the grace of humility and small-ness, the grace never to discourage myself over my limits or my errors and always to put all my trust in God.

Light from a Faithful Witness

"Nothing troubles us so much as self-love and self-regard. [. . .] Why are we troubled to find that we have committed a sin or even an imperfection? Because we thought ourselves to be something good, firm, and solid. And therefore, when we have seen the proof to the contrary, and have fallen on our faces in the dirt, we are troubled, offended, and anxious. If we understood ourselves, we would be astonished that we are ever able to remain standing."

—St. Francis de Sales

"You would have Peace, in spite of everything, if you knew how to see the divine will or divine permission even in your miseries, and especially if, convinced that infinite love presides over everything here below, you understood the role that your miseries so preciously play in the work of your spiritual progress."[1]

—Fr. Marie-Étienne Vayssière, OP

"If you want to find rest, do not compare yourself to others."

—St. Teresa Benedicta of the Cross, OCD

MEDITATE ON THE WORD

I meditate on this passage from Psalm 131:

> O Lord, my heart is not lifted up, my eyes are not raised too high; I do not occupy myself with things too great and too marvelous for me. But I have calmed and quieted my soul, like a child quieted at its mother's breast; like a child that is quieted is my soul. O Israel, hope in the Lord from this time forth and for evermore (Verse:1–3).

---

1. Marie-Étienne Vayssière, *Consentir à l'amour: Lettres choisies* (Consent to Love: Selected Letters), (Burtin, France: Éditions des Béatitudes, 2018), p. 130.

I keep this verse in my heart, this verse that I repeat often during the day:

"I have calmed and quieted my soul, like a child quieted at its mother's breast; like a child that is quieted is my soul."

Seventh Day

NO FORGIVENESS, NO PEACE

Daily Meditation

INVITATION TO CONTEMPLATION

I compose myself, present to the current moment, and I breathe calmly. With the eyes of faith, I put myself in God's view, that of the Father of Heaven who loves me tenderly. I am attentive to God's presence in my heart. I contemplate for several minutes.

SIGN OF THE CROSS

In the name of the Father, and of the Son, and of the Holy Spirit. Amen.

PRAYER TO THE HOLY SPIRIT

Holy Spirit, you who are the light, you who are the consoler, come guide my prayer this day. Make me know the beauty and depth of divine love. Come establish God's peace in my heart and make me capable of spreading this peace around me.

MEDITATION FROM
FR. JACQUES PHILIPPE

If we want to have true interior peace, one necessary condition is to forgive those who have wronged us.

Forgiveness obviously isn't easy when someone deeply hurts us. It sometimes takes a lot of time to forgive. We ask for this grace humbly in prayer because it's often beyond our strength. We should begin by wanting to forgive and asking God for this grace in humble and persevering prayer. We must turn towards the Father, the only one who is capable of forgiveness because he is the only one who can heal and restore everything. The source of forgiveness isn't in ourselves, it is in God. Like Jesus, we must address ourselves to God in these terms: "Father, forgive them; for they know not what they do" (Lk 23:34).

If we ask with perseverance and faith, one day the grace will be given to us to be able to pardon with our full heart, and this will be a source of peace. We will sense that love has finally triumphed in our heart, that we have come out of our narrowness of thought and judgment, and that we have become free to respond to misfortune with love, free to overcome evil with good, as St. Paul says (see Rom 12:21).

We will become capable of considering the other not as an enemy but as a brother. This experience will make love's victory possible and will put us in a great peace.

If, on the other hand, we refuse to forgive, if we harden ourselves and close our hearts to whoever did us wrong, we will always be holding onto grudges, resentment, and bad thoughts towards the wrong-doer.

These thoughts and feelings take up a lot of space in our hearts, and prevent them from tasting this profound peace.

A heart can't feel enduring peace unless love reigns in it. So long as it is inhabited by hate, resentment, or bad thoughts towards others, it's impossible for love to reign.

We should also be aware of the following: If I've been hurt by someone who did me wrong, it's only on the day when I finally decide to forgive that person that my heart can begin the path of deep healing and peace. If someone has made me their victim, nourishing grudges against that person won't make me any better, much less would doing something bad to the person. I can only be healed through forgiveness and mercy. "Blessed are the merciful, for they will obtain mercy" (Mt 5:7).

The decision to forgive isn't always easy, but it's the only choice that will lead to full healing.

To succeed at forgiveness, we must understand that the decision to forgive is based on faith and hope.

Faith gives us the ability to believe that God is powerful enough to make good out of the evil we've suffered, allowing us to surpass the angry and resentful feelings against the other. If we are certain, thanks to faith, that God is capable of giving us more than we've lost because of others' faults, the reasons to be angry with those others disappear little by little.

To forgive is also an act of hope towards the person who has wronged me. Forgiving means that I don't want to enclose this person in the wrong committed, but that I believe in a possible conversion. Not forgiving means the contrary, condemning the person in a definitive manner, negating all possibility of true repentance and conversion. Do we have the right to do this? God never loses hope for anyone, and we must imitate him.

Forgiveness means no longer seeing the person as a definite enemy, but leaving the door open to a possible reconciliation. Of course, it doesn't just depend on me alone, but the simple act of leaving the door open through forgiveness to a future where love triumphs instead of evil, which will give me peace. Each time that I practice faith and hope, peace grows.

Prayer

Let us put our trust in the Virgin Mary, the Queen of Peace:

> Hail Mary, full of grace, the Lord is with thee. Blessed art thou among women and blessed is the fruit of thy womb, Jesus. Holy Mary, Mother of God, pray for us, sinners, now and at the hour of our death. Amen.

May the all-powerful and merciful God bless us and keep us, he who is Father, Son and Holy Spirit. Amen.

A GRACE TO REQUEST

I ask myself this question: who are the people that I still despise today? I ask God for the grace to be able to forgive them with all my heart, and I entrust them to the mercy of God.

LIGHT FROM A FAITHFUL WITNESS

"Learn the art of war on yourself; on others, the art of peace."

—Ven. Madeleine Delbrêl

MEDITATE ON THE WORD

In the Letter to the Colossians, St. Paul says this:

[Forbear] one another and, if one has a complaint against another, [forgive] each other; as the Lord has forgiven you, so you also must forgive. And above all these put on love, which binds everything together in perfect harmony. And let the peace of Christ rule in your hearts, to which indeed you were called in the one body (Col 3:13–15).

I remember this phrase and repeat it often during my day:

"As the Lord has forgiven you, so you also must forgive."

Eighth Day

To Find Peace,
Accept Life as It Is

Daily Meditation

INVITATION TO CONTEMPLATION

I compose myself, present to the current moment, and I breathe calmly. With the eyes of faith, I put myself in God's view, that of the Father of Heaven who loves me tenderly. I am attentive to God's presence in my heart. I contemplate for several minutes.

SIGN OF THE CROSS

In the name of the Father, and of the Son, and of the Holy Spirit. Amen.

PRAYER TO THE HOLY SPIRIT

Holy Spirit, you who are the light, you who are the consoler, come guide my prayer this day. Make me know the beauty and depth of divine love. Come establish God's peace in my heart and make me capable of spreading this peace around me.

MEDITATION FROM
FR. JACQUES PHILIPPE

One of the conditions for finding peace may be the most difficult to practice—it's saying "yes" to everything that happens to us, which includes beautiful, gratifying things, but also difficulties and suffering of all sorts that we might encounter. This practice may appear very shocking because it isn't in keeping with the modern mentality. Indeed, mankind would rather become the master of everything and mold reality to meet all its desires!

The attitude of acceptance, however, requires great faith: We must believe, in the end, that everything is from God's hands, believing also that all reality that seems *theoretically* negative for us can one day become positive.

This act of faith is what Scripture invites us to do.

Job puts it this way: We receive happiness as a gift from God, why not also receive misfortune? (See Job 2:10).

St. James, in the beginning of his letter, even goes as far as saying "Count it all joy, my brethren, when you meet various trials" (Jas 1:2).

To find peace, we must then accept with faith everything that happens in our lives: joys as well as consternations. Obviously, it's not about becoming passive. We must try to eliminate as much as possible of the suffering and evil present in the world. But we know very well that whatever our capacity or efforts are, there still will be a lot of sorrowful situations where we find ourselves powerless. What to do, then? Revolt, get discouraged, or despair? No, but abandon ourselves with trust to the arms of God in accepting reality as it is, and not as we dream it would be.

Accepting the faith is not about being fatalistic, either, nor about attributing everything that happens in the world to divine will. There are a lot of things that happen that God doesn't desire. Nevertheless, in a mysterious way, he permits them, and if he permits them, it's because he can draw a good thing out of them. That's where his wisdom and strength is revealed. God can draw good out of evil. We don't have a mathematical proof of it; it's an act of faith that we are invited to make, truly a leap of faith that we have to experience.

But it's exactly this type of act of faith that's a little bit crazy that Jesus invites us to make in the Gospel. Remember how he said, "Don't be afraid," "Don't fear men," "Don't be worried about anything," and "In the world you have tribulation, but be of good cheer, I have overcome the world"? St. Paul affirms Jesus' reassurance, saying, "in everything God works for good with those who love him" (Rom 8:28).

If we don't have this perspective, we will always be at war with life, we will be angry, disappointed, sad, or discouraged each time things don't go our way, and we will never be at peace. It's in accepting what is real, in accepting our share of the cross and its sign of contradiction where we will inevitably find peace. When we welcome the trial, when we accept the chalice presented to us instead of pushing it aside, we finish by finding peace. It's a very surprising experience.

If we act this way, with a real act of faith in God's fidelity, then we will experience how the trials and tribulations finally become positive. The troubles will oblige us to know ourselves better in truth, to see our radical poverty, and to throw out our illusions and our narrow-minded wisdom.

Trials change our outlook on ourselves, on life, on others. When accepted with faith, they lead us to profound conversions that ultimately are revealed as beneficial. They make us experience in a very concrete way how God is faithful, how he is merciful, and how he can make good come of all things.

PRAYER

Let us put our trust in the Virgin Mary, the Queen of Peace:

> Hail Mary, full of grace, the Lord is with thee. Blessed art thou among women and blessed is the fruit of thy womb, Jesus. Holy Mary, Mother of God, pray for us, sinners, now and at the hour of our death. Amen.

May the all-powerful and merciful God bless us and keep us, he who is Father, Son and Holy Spirit. Amen.

A Grace to Request

I ask myself this question: What is the thing in my life that I have the most difficulty accepting today? I ask God for the grace to accept this reality with faith, believing that God can make good come out of it.

Light from a Faithful Witness

"Put all your efforts not into being something, but into being only what God wants, only because God wants it. Peace, very quickly, will be your share."[1]

—Fr. Marie-Étienne Vayssière, OP

"We must live in peace and not worry about what God doesn't seem to want for us. Knowing

---

1. Marie-Étienne Vayssière, *Consentir à l'amour: Lettres choisies* (Consent to Love: Selected Letters) (Burtin, France: Éditions des Béatitudes, 2018),p. 181.

how to wait a very long time for divine gifts or for relief from a burden, and living peacefully, is the end of all ends because it's a completely filial attitude. Everything turns out well for the one who loves God."

—Fr. Jerome

Meditate on the Word

In the Letter to the Romans, St. Paul says this:

We know that in everything God works for good with those who love him, who are called according to his purpose (Rom 8:28).

I memorize this sentence and repeat it often during the day:

"We know that in everything God works for good with those who love him."

Ninth Day

To Find Peace, Live in the Present Moment

Daily Meditation

INVITATION TO CONTEMPLATION

I compose myself, present to the current moment, and I breathe calmly. With the eyes of faith, I put myself in God's view, that of the Father of Heaven who loves me tenderly. I am attentive to God's presence in my heart. I contemplate for several minutes.

SIGN OF THE CROSS

In the name of the Father, and of the Son, and of the Holy Spirit. Amen.

PRAYER TO THE HOLY SPIRIT

Holy Spirit, you who are the light, you who are the consoler, come guide my prayer this day. Make me know the beauty and depth of divine love. Come establish God's peace in my heart and make me capable of spreading this peace around me.

MEDITATION FROM
FR. JACQUES PHILIPPE

We'll meditate on the final attitude that encourages interior peace during this last day of our retreat. It is "living in the present moment."

A great enemy of interior peace is this tendency we often have to return to our past or to project into the future. This tendency most often creates a lot of troubles and worries.

If we want to accept God's peace, we must remain in the present moment as much as possible, entrusting our past to God's infinite mercy, and putting our future in the hands of his providence. We must do whatever we have to do today, without letting the regrets of the past or fears of the future weigh on our lives.

This isn't easy. Our spirit is too mobile. Instead of simply worrying about what we have to do today and fully investing ourselves in it, we often turn our thoughts and imagination to the past or the future.

It's good, of course, to return to the past sometimes whether to draw lessons from it and avoid falling into the same errors, or to ask forgiveness or give forgiveness where necessary, or to entrust an old wound to God which we haven't given up fully, yet. But we must adamantly avoid ruminating on the past, tormenting ourselves with regrets or remorse. Once we have asked God for forgiveness for our faults, we have put them in the hands of the Father; it's not necessary to come back to them. We should even become certain that he can make good come out of them. Nothing is impossible for God. He can even make good come from our errors.

The past matters little, then. It's very important to abandon it completely into the hands of God We must be resolved to live today with trust, to love, and to apply ourselves to whatever our vocation requires of us at the present moment. And to begin again each morning with the same hope.

It's good to learn to live one day at a time, especially in difficult times. We learn to apply ourselves to whatever we have to do today, without wanting to solve all our life's problems, without trying to remake the past or assure the future. "Tomorrow will be anxious for itself," as the Gospel says (see Mt 6:34) .

Avoid projecting onto the future, either by trying to imagine what it will be like and wanting to program it in some way or another, or by trying to resolve in advance the problems that may never materialize.

What we project onto the future the majority of times is worry.

What will tomorrow bring? What will I become in ten years? We lose a lot of time and energy preoccupying ourselves with these concerns. Instead, we should content ourselves with doing what's necessary for today, trusting our future to divine providence, just as Jesus invites us to do in the Gospel. Remember his words:

> So do not worry and say, "What are we to eat?"or "What are we to drink?" or "What are we to wear?" All these things the pagans seek. Your heavenly Father knows that you need them all. But seek first the kingdom [of God] and his righteousness, and all these things will be given you besides. Do not worry about tomorrow; tomorrow will take care of itself.

Sufficient for a day is its own evil (Mt 6:31–34, NABRE translation).

It's not about turning a blind eye or becoming irresponsible. Sometimes we do need to think about the future and prepare for it. But what we should avoid at all cost is the worry and the fear. These concerns upset us and stop us from being available for how we need to live today, being present to God, to ourselves, and to others. "You must be occupied, but not preoccupied," St. Maximilian Kolbe said. Love and charity will thus win over all.

PRAYER

Let us put our trust in the Virgin Mary, the Queen of Peace:

Hail Mary, full of grace, the Lord is with thee. Blessed art thou among women and blessed is the fruit of thy womb, Jesus. Holy Mary, Mother of God, pray for us, sinners, now and at the hour of our death. Amen.

May the all-powerful and merciful God bless us and keep us, he who is Father, Son and Holy Spirit. Amen.

A GRACE TO REQUEST

I place my whole past into God's hands anew, with the trust that he can draw good from anything. I entrust my future to him, and only ask for the grace to do well what is asked of me today.

LIGHT FROM A FAITHFUL WITNESS

"Only look at and worry for the present moment, seeing it in his infinite love for you and always welcoming it such as it is in trust and peace."[1]

—Fr. Marie-Étienne Vayssière, OP

"My past, O Lord, to your mercy, my present to your Love, my future to your Providence."

—St. Pio of Pietrelcina (Padre Pio)

---

1. Marie-Étienne Vayssière, *Consentir à l'amour: Lettres choisies* (Consent to Love: Selected Letters), (Burtin, France: Éditions des Béatitudes, 2018), p. 37.

MEDITATE ON THE WORD

I re-read Jesus's words in the Gospel of Matthew.

> So do not worry and say, "What are we to eat?"
> or "What are we to drink?" or "What are we to
> wear?" All these things the pagans seek. Your
> heavenly Father knows that you need them
> all. But seek first the kingdom [of God] and
> his righteousness, and all these things will be
> given you besides. Do not worry about tomor-
> row; tomorrow will take care of itself. Suffi-
> cient for a day is its own evil (Mt 6:31–34).

I keep these words in my heart, repeating often
during the day:

"Do not worry about tomorrow; tomorrow
will take care of itself. Sufficient for a day is its
own evil."